Quick Project Management For Beginners!

Project Management

Influence, Lead, And Manage Your Team For Increased Productivity And Performance

Mick McPherson

STOP!!! Before you read any further....Would you like to know the Secrets of Transforming your life, overcome insecurities, develop leadership skills, and undeniable confidence in your personal, professional, and relationship life?

If your answer is yes, then you are not alone. Thousands of people are looking for the secret to have unstoppable confidence and self-driven power in all areas of their lives.

If you have been searching for these answers without much luck, you're in the right place!

Not only will you gain incredible insight in this book, but because I want to make sure to give you as much value as possible, right now for a limited time you can get full **100% FREE access to a VIP bonus EBook** entitled **LIMITLESS ENERGY!**

Just Go Here For Free Instant Access:

www.PotentialRise.com

Legal Notice

Disclaimer Notice

information contained herein on the new conditions whenever they see applicable.

Table Of Contents

Introduction

I want to thank you and congratulate you for purchasing the book, *"Project Management: Quick Project Management For Beginners! - Influence, Lead, And Manage Your Team For Increased Productivity And Performance!"*

This "Project Management" book contains proven steps and strategies on how to become a good project manager. This involves knowing the basics of making an effective project plan, how to manage time effectively, manage risks, monitor the performance of your team members, and different qualities that a project manager should possess.

Most organizations do not have enough time to get their employees working on projects, compelling them to rely on third party project management teams to do the job for them. This explains why the project management field is progressing these days, and why some people want to become project managers of certain teams. However, project management is not a simple task. It involves working on producing numerous outputs at any given time, managing teams that are formed solely for the project and are not really bonded together, and lastly dealing with contingencies so that the group will be able to deliver what is expected of them. This implies that if the project manager is not competent enough for the position, the project will ultimately end in failure.

With the help of this book, aspiring project managers will know the basics of the field that they want to be in and prepare for what they will be experiencing once they're managing their own project team.

Thanks again for purchasing this book. I hope you enjoy it!

Chapter 1 - The Basics Of Project Management

Every organization has numerous tasks that should be accomplished; some tasks have longer durations, and may need to be constantly taken care of, while others are short-lived and are only introduced because the need for it arose. These short term tasks are also known as projects. But even if projects are temporary tasks that need to be carried out, it doesn't mean that they should be attended to unsystematically. There is a proper method that should be followed if you want a good outcome for the project that should be accomplished.

This chapter will discuss basic information about project management.

Defining points of project management

In this chapter's introduction, the term project management was given a brief definition. But aside from having a general idea as to what this concept is about, it's also important that the different points surrounding project management are defined. It is only by specifying these points that we will truly understand what this concept is.

These factors are as follows:

- Project management has an exact beginning and end – projects are simply temporary tasks that the organization needs to be accomplished and delivered before the deadline. To differentiate it from regular work, projects are usually not repeatable; if ever it will have to be repeated, this usually happens after a significant amount of time has passed.

- Project management is an independent work – another

difference between regular work at an organization and projects is that the former usually relies on the output of other departments, whereas the latter is independent. This simply means that even if the project team was not able to deliver the task assigned to it, other departments can carry out their work and will not affect their performance.

- Project managements utilize different tools to identify the tasks that were accomplished and the progress of the whole team compared to the time that they still have – in order for project managers to determine if they are on the right track and if they can accomplish the said task within the specified time frame, they use different tools to measure success. Some of these tools are Gantt and PERT charts, and a Work Breakdown table that is based on the objectives created before the project starts.

- Project management increases the probability of a task to turn out as successful – project managers look at all angles to determine the risks and possible problems that they may experience while doing the task. This will obviously result in devising a good plan so that the objectives can be met and the task will be delivered successfully.

Three factors for successful project management

For project management to become successful, there are three general factors that every team should consider:

- Time – as mentioned, projects follow a specified schedule and should be delivered before that deadline comes. Otherwise, the outcome of the project may be unused.

- Scope – the project should follow certain boundaries so that the outcome is specialized for the department or organization that requested for the task. For example, if you are asked to provide an architectural blueprint for a commercial building, make sure that the end product will not look like something else.

- Cost – just like time, most projects have a certain budget to cover the expenses needed for its accomplishment. All project managers strive to deliver the project successfully while using the least amount of resources.

Now that you have learned about the definition of project management and what factors should be present in order for it to become successful, the focus will now be shifted to the actual process of project management.

Chapter 2 - 6 Essential Steps Of Project Management For Beginners

Just as the term project management suggests, any project can only be successful if there is a system being followed for its implementation. Although the steps that should be applied for each project greatly vary, there is a pattern that can be used so that management becomes successful.

This chapter will discuss the 6 important steps that aspiring project managers should observe so that they will be successful with their task.

Project specifications

The first step in project management revolves on identifying or defining different factors that could influence the project's turnout. These factors are the following:

- Goals and objectives – before actions can be implemented, the project driver (person or organization in need of the project) specifies what he wants or is expecting the team to accomplish. After knowing the goals of the project driver, the project managers will then identify the objectives that they should reach in order for the "big picture" need of the project driver to be fulfilled.

- Identifying the milestones of each objective – upon identifying the objectives, it is also necessary to determine how performance can be measured. By identifying a quota or performance indicators, project managers can tell if the next step should be taken or not.

Project set-up

Just as the term suggests, this step covers the preparation that should be engaged by the project team so that work will be done continuously once they started implementing the steps needed to accomplish every objective. This includes identifying things that should be bought or people that should be hired in order for the project to be successfully carried out.

Planning stage

Upon identifying the specifics in the first step, the next stage will focus on identifying the steps that should be taken in order for the objectives to be met. This is also when the process that should be followed in order to achieve the objectives are formulated. The process as well as the materials/people needed for the project has to comply with the limitations of time, resources, and scope specified by the project driver. This stage can also be used to specify the steps that can be taken if ever problems are encountered during the implementation stage.

Project implementation

This is the stage wherein the people who are part of the project team are instructed to work so that the service or product will be delivered to the project driver.

Project control and supervision

Once the team starts working, the manager needs to make sure that the objectives are being met according to schedule and that the whole project will be delivered before the deadline. It is also in this stage that any corrective actions are applied to people who may cause a delay on the project's delivery.

Project termination

The team assembled to accomplish the project is disbanded. However, this will only happen if the expected product or service is successfully delivered and has satisfied the project driver's expectation.

Chapter 3 - Get Stuff Done! Know How To Make An Effective Project Plan

It was mentioned in the previous chapter that planning is one of the tasks that project managers should accomplish if they want to deliver what is expected of them. This will serve as the basis of all team activities and can be used to measure their success.

This chapter will give you an idea as to what makes a good project plan.

The project plan should have goals patterned from the needs of stakeholders

 The first step to make your own project plan should start with identifying the stakeholders as well as formulating project goals that are based on their needs.

A stakeholder is somebody who will experience the impact if the particular project is delivered. The most common stakeholders are the project drivers, the users of the product or output, the customers, and the whole project team.

Upon knowing the stakeholders, their needs should also be identified. This can be done by utilizing various methods such as interviews and surveys. The stakeholder's needs should be prioritized accordingly, as this is where the goals and your objectives of the project will come from. Make sure that goals follow the SMART principle, as this will make it easier to track progress.

Identify the deliverables of your project

Once goals are identified, the next step involves specifying the things that should be produced by the project team so that the goals will be met. The deliverables should not be mistaken with the finished product or final output. Most project managers expect different deliverables within a specified time, and all of which are important in accomplishing the final deliverable.

Identify the requirements so that deliverables can be provided

Whether the deliverable is a tangible product or an abstract output, you need to know what the project team should have so that the deliverables will be provided to their stakeholders. If any equipment, ingredient, or manpower is needed, the plan should contain details as to where these can be obtained.

Contingency plans

Even with the most careful planning, it is somehow impossible to get everything to work in your favor. Assume that some of the processes that you have formulated will fail. Once they do, you need to have a back-up plan so that the team can continue to work in achieving your goals without getting the production interrupted. By having contingency plans, you will be able to save time and money.

Consider the help of the whole team

Even as the project manager, you need to make sure that team members are involved in the whole planning process. This is especially true if some of your team members are experts or are experienced on the task that will be accomplished. This will allow you to formulate more efficient plans so that the project will end successfully.

Chapter 4 - Time Management Tips To Get More Work Done

It was mentioned in the previous chapters that time is one of the limited resources that project managers should always consider. This is why it is imperative that the leaders of the project know how to manage time properly and deliver the task within the schedule.

This chapter will provide time management tips that can be used by aspiring project managers so that they can get more work done while taking the least amount of time.

Identify all important factors related to the project as early as possible

The first three steps of project management involve the identification of all important elements that should be present so that the project can be accomplished without delays. By specifying the objectives and breaking the steps so that it will be easier for team members to accomplish, identifying the milestones for the project and performance indicators for each step, and getting all necessary materials within reach, the project can be finished before the specified time.

Meetings should be held to collect ideas and think of solutions

One time-consuming mistake that starting project managers commit is that they call for a meeting with the purpose of identifying any issues or problems experienced by the team members as well as asking for updates from each group assigned with a specific task. While this action fosters upward communication, the time for meetings can be better used if members are involved of thinking for solutions. Identify the problems beforehand, as this will be the focus of your meetings.

Make sure that meetings, just like the tasks, should not exceed the time allotted for it. This will still give you enough time to accomplish the work related to the project itself.

Refrain from micro-managing

Delving too much on the results of each group based on what is acceptable for you should be avoided, as it will only waste time. Use the performance indicators and objectives formulated during the first few phases of project management so that the quality of work will not be judged based on your preference. After all, the end product is made for and will be used by the project driver.

Apply the 80/20 principle

The Pareto (80/20) principle is proven to foster efficiency in any task. This principle simply states that only 20% of the activities contribute to 80% of the project's progress. Thus, your goal as a project manager is to identify what these activities are and making sure that they are done effectively and efficiently. By doing so, you will experience drastic improvements on the performance of team members and on the progress of the project. This can also be used to identify what should be on your to-do list for each day.

Chapter 5 - Project Risk Management For Beginners

Every action that we take involves risk. Even the simple act of walking carries the risk of being tripped and getting injured. The same is true with projects. If these risks are not managed, it will result in the team's inability to deliver the work expected of them.

This chapter will identify project risk management and provide useful tips that aspiring risk managers can apply.

Project manager's qualities for effective risk management

In order to manage risk effectively, project managers should possess the following qualities:

Identifying risk is a constant job

Aside from identifying the goals and objectives of the project, the risk that can be faced once it starts should also be included on the things that should be identified by the project manager. This allows them to formulate contingency plans and back-up actions that can be taken if ever these unfortunate events occur. However, risk management is different from the goals and objectives. This is because the former usually not change as the project progresses, whereas the latter does not. Even if you have identified the steps that should be taken to accomplish the project, some risks that were not foreseen at the start may occur during the implementation stage. This simply implies that project managers cannot be complacent even if they have determined the risks and thought of their solutions before the start of the project. Risks can occur any time, and it is the job of project managers to observe the whole process and look for such until the project is terminated.

But even if other risks can be experienced after the project starts, it doesn't mean that you should skip on identifying it as early as possible. The risks that you can identify at the start are usually the main risks that could seriously impede the progress of the project. By being able to identify them before the steps are applied, it will be easier to overcome the problems once they arise in the middle of project implementation.

Do not be afraid of discussing about risks

Project managers have the task of consulting with group leaders so that they can be updated with the progress of the task that they're assigned with. But aside from asking for updates, you also have to identify the risks that the leaders foresee for their group. Having "first hand" experience in the department, they can provide more concrete information and solution to the problem rather than just considering the views of somebody watching from the sidelines. This will help prevent failure in any of the groups and ultimately, prevent the whole project group to fail their tasks.

Prioritize the risks that you identified

Once the risks are identified, it is also necessary to arrange these risks accordingly. The hierarchy should be based on the effect that one risk has over the whole process. Thus, risks that could greatly impact the project should be attended to first, while those with the least impact should be placed lower in the hierarchy.

Risk management techniques

Aside from possessing the necessary qualities that project managers should have to minimize risks, several methods can also be applied so that it can be reduced further. These techniques are the following:

- Risk acceptance – this method of risk management technique involves the project manager to continue with the action even with the presence of the risk. This is similar to the example pointed out in this chapter's introduction.

- Risk controlling – somehow similar to risk acceptance, as the action is still carried out even when risk is present. However, risk controlling involves the development of a plan to reduce the risk and tracking if the plan is successful with its goal. With risk controlling, this is where formulating plans with the help of experienced individuals is applied.

- Risk avoidance – this method involves doing the opposite of the behavior that carries the risk. For example, if you do not want to trip because of walking, you will rather stay immobile or move from one place to another without walking (such as using a wheel chair). While this method is not always possible to apply (as some risks should be taken in order to experience high gains), it is considered to be an effective technique on situations where it can be applied.

Risk transfer – in this method, the project management team or driver forces another party to accept the risk such as hedging or requiring the other party to sign a contract. For example, shippers should not be held responsible for the delivery of the product once they are in the hands of the courier, since the products are in good condition prior to packaging and delivery.

Chapter 6 - Leadership Qualities Of An Effective Project Manager

Just like businesses or organizations, project teams are lead by somebody whose purpose is to ensure that the group is able to deliver the job that is expected of it. However, for you to become an effective leader, you have to possess certain qualities.

This chapter will identify the qualities that a project manager should possess so that he can steer the group towards success.

The project manager should be passionate about learning

Every project is an opportunity for the manager to learn something new. Even if the steps that should be followed to construct a good action plan and you follow a certain routine for the whole project, you must be open to generating new ideas and acquiring more knowledge so that you will be the go-to person of the whole group. By having sufficient knowledge about the project, formulating steps, contingencies, and managing risks will be easier. You also get to take home the experience that you can use for the next projects that you will be managing, making you better at what you do.

A project manager should be committed

An individual who is committed to the work that is assigned to them are more responsible, which obviously translates into positive behavior. A committed project manager is one who is willing to work in every aspect of the project, and will mostly act as if they are the project driver. This positivity and eagerness to complete the work could spell the difference between an acceptable and a great product or outcome.

The project manager knows how to delegate tasks

effectively

Being the leader of the project team, one of your tasks is to spread the work to be done among the members of the group so that they will be accomplished. However, delegating tasks can only be effective if you are able to match the correct people to do them. This will give your members the idea that you trust them enough to accomplish the task, and that they are the only one who can provide the quality of work that you're expecting.

Effective delegation also involves mutual agreement between you and the group or individual whom the task was assigned. This can be reached by specifying the work to be done, the quality of work that should be produced, asking for an estimate as to when the tasks can be completed, and agreeing on the dates where progress updates should be provided to you.

The project manager should be willing to take calculated risks

It was mentioned in the previous chapter that project managers should do their best in minimizing risks so that the team can successfully deliver the expected output. However, this doesn't mean that project managers should avoid all risks. Remember that it is also their job to identify which risks should be accepted or controlled, and which should be avoided or transferred.

When a project manager takes calculated risks, this simply means that the cost of taking the risk when they failed is less than the benefits that they can get if they become successful by doing it. They have also devised a plan that will be applied if ever they're unsuccessful while taking the risk. By being able to take calculated risks, this will prove that you're willing to go beyond your limits and "think outside the box" so that better results can be experienced.

Chapter 7 - Monitoring Your Team's Performance

The purpose of the project plan is to help the project manager in identifying the progress of the team. It is also used to qualify if the end result provided by each group complies with the standards that were set during the planning stage.

In this chapter, we will enumerate certain practices that project managers should adapt so that they can effectively monitor the progress and performance of their team.

Make sure that the plan is updated regularly

One destructive assumption that many project managers have regarding the project plan is that once it is checked and approved by the project drivers, they can simply stick to it as a guide and not change it as the project progresses. While project plans should be as accurate as possible when they're submitted so that sudden changes will be avoided, it's impossible to predict everything correctly. Depending on the pace of the project's accomplishment, the project plan should also be modified. By doing so, the chances of successfully delivering the project's output is improved.

Check if the team is able to follow the time frame

Since the time given to project groups is often limited, they need to make sure that their progress is right on schedule. As a project manager, your duty is to regularly check the status of activities once a specified amount of time has passed. This also involves meeting with group leaders, as they can give a more accurate feedback regarding the activity being ahead, behind, or just on schedule. Additionally, leaders can provide suggestions that can be implemented so that the work can be done faster.

Monitor the project's budget

Aside from taking note of how much time was already spent, the amount of money spent and how much still remains should also be taken note of. And even if you have submitted an estimate on your initial project plan, it is recommended to continuously check if the costs can be reduced for the remaining days that the project will be made.

Make sure that the team's activities are within the scope

As the project continues, some tasks may need to be added so that it can be successfully delivered. However, you have to make sure that what the team is doing follows the scope that was specified in the initial project plan. If the activity is necessary but not included on the scope, you can consider including it as part of the project's scope.

Chapter 8 - Get Increased Productivity By Formulating Feasible Project Schedules

Since project teams are given limited time to work on their output, they need to be able to accomplish their deliverables as quick as possible. This is why schedules are part of the project plan.

This chapter will provide you with a basic guide so that your proposed project schedule will be easy to attain.

Identify all activities as early as possible

It's necessary to know all tasks relevant to the project before the implementation phase, as it will greatly help you in allocating an ample amount of time for it to be accomplished.

Activities should be broken down into simpler tasks

Once the activities are determined, your next step should be to break it down to simpler tasks. Not only will these tasks be more specific for the assigned member, it will also be easier to monitor the progress of the whole activity.

Consider the order and duration of the task

Tasks are different, both in order (that which should be accomplished first before another task can be engaged in) and the duration (how much time is needed to work on it). It is the project manager's duty to identify which tasks are most important or is considered as "prerequisites", well as to know which of them needs more time before it can be accomplished.

Identify the steps that you will utilize before the duration is allocated

In order to give a better estimate as to the amount of time needed to accomplish the activities, you need to first specify the strategy that you will be applying for each. This will prevent you from giving the members too much time to work on the task and risk wasting it before another activity is started. Likewise, this will prevent too little time allocation, which could greatly affect the quality of their performance.

Identify all risks and contingency plans, and how much time is needed for them

Aside from the duration of the methods used to carry out the task, you also need to identify the duration of the contingency plan if ever Plan A fails. This should also be included on your project schedule before you move on to another activity. This will give you enough time to carry out your Plan B without messing the whole schedule and falling behind.

Chapter 9 - How To Manage Your Team When Conflicts Arise

Teams may be working for a single purpose, but it is still composed of individuals whose traits vary from one person to another. These differences can be the cause of conflicts. Unfortunately, project teams cannot afford to let conflicts unresolved, as it can seriously affect the final output's quality and delivery.

This chapter will provide the steps that you can follow in order to settle conflicts between team members as early as possible.

Listen and acknowledge what the conflicting parties have to say

Small conflicts can get worse because none of the parties are listening to what the other has to say. As the project manager and mediator, you need to listen to the message that each team member wants to convey. Aside from that, you also have to acknowledge, or let the individual know that what they're saying is being heard even if their point of view is different from what you have.

Respond based on what the other person has said

To foster better communication, you need to respond after the other party finished saying what they have to say. But rather than making an antagonistic response if their point of view is different from yours, you should provide feedbacks that are constructive and present alternative solutions that they could consider. Additionally, you can provide personal experiences and explanations so that they will see why you are disagreeing with them.

Once you have responded, make sure to be open about possible challenges to your point of view. Aside from being able to improve communication, it will also help you to see things through their perspective if they are allowed to explain their thoughts further.

Resolve other problems that arose from the initial discourse

While the conflict may have started with a few issues, the initial dialogue is an opportunity to look at other points which are yet to cause conflict but has a tendency to become one if left unresolved. Additionally, this is an opportunity to tackle issues that may have caused the conflict to arise. This involves looking at the situation in full detail and identifying how it can be solved one small step at a time. By doing so, the possibility of experiencing conflicts and having delays at work will be significantly reduced. This will ultimately give your team members more time to focus on their tasks and be able to achieve their goals.

Conflicts are not always bad. Sometimes, it can be used as an opportunity to change the current system so that the team will be more efficient in delivering the work that is expected from them.

Chapter 10 - Effective Team Building Strategies For Project Managers

In order for the project team to produce the output expected of them, they need to be able to work together. Otherwise, they will not be able to accomplish the task and provide the deliverables in time.

This chapter will identify some of the basic team building strategies that should be applied by project managers in order to get the group to work together.

Have a uniform and clear goal

For your team to be successful, their actions should be towards meeting a single and clear goal. It will be difficult to follow through the efforts of one group and produce the expected output if the work of other groups is not directed towards achieving the same goal.

Members should be part of a group where their skills are needed

If a group member is good at a particular field, you have to make sure that they are placed in a group where other people have the same skill or strength. Not only is it helpful in getting more work done in less time, the chances of members getting in conflict with one another due to one person's lack of skills is significantly reduced. This can also get members to be interested in working with the group, as their environment can be used as a testing ground to measure their skills and to learn from people who have more experience.

Make sure to communicate constantly

Misunderstandings between different groups and members can be minimized if there is an avenue where they can communicate with one another. Work efficiency can still be achieved even when communicating, since there are many tools that help us stay connected with other project team members. Just make sure that these channels are used properly, as uncontrolled communication may cause members to procrastinate and focus more on socialization than work.

Conclusion

Managing a project, even a short-lived activity, involves the skills that managers at an organization should possess. By knowing how to do the job correctly, you will surely get through your projects successfully and, in turn, significantly contribute to the progress of your career

Thank you again for purchasing this book on project management!

I am extremely excited to pass this information along to you, and I am so happy that you now have read and can hopefully implement these strategies going forward.

I hope this book was able to help you understand what project management is in a nutshell and how to become an effective leader for a temporary team made to fulfill a specific goal.

The next step is to get started using this information and to hopefully live a life of successful career and management of tasks as well as of people!

Please don't be someone who just reads this information and doesn't apply it, the strategies in this book will only benefit you if you use them!

If you know of anyone else that could benefit from the information presented here please inform them of this book.

Finally, if you enjoyed this book and feel it has added value to your life in any way, please take the time to share your thoughts and post a review on Amazon. It'd be greatly appreciated!

Thank you and good luck!

Preview Of:

Ultimate Accelerated Learning Techniques!

<u>Accelerated Learning</u>

Best Accelerated Learning Tips To Improve Memory And Speed Reading, Enhance Intellect And Brain Power, And To Learn More Faster!

Introduction

I want to thank you and congratulate you for purchasing the book, *"Accelerated Learning: Ultimate Accelerated Learning Techniques! - Best Accelerated Learning Tips To Improve Memory And Speed Reading, Enhance Intellect And Brain Power, And To Learn More Faster!"*

This "Accelerated Learning" book contains proven steps and strategies on how to learn things faster using minimal effort. Thanks to the current studies that link the nature of the human brain to the learning process; there are concepts and methodologies that could be used to boost man's capacity to learn more.

While there are already solid educational psychology laws that govern and explain the process of learning in humans, there are researchers who still want to push on into the realms of "hyper learning". Traditional methods of teaching and learning are effective up to this day. However, the advancements in society and technology deem it necessary that the new generation of learners keep up.

There are many approaches to speed up the learning process. This will depend upon the background of the one who is aiming towards it. Psychologists, teachers, neurologists, and even child development experts have different techniques to share when it comes to boosting up the rate of learning within individuals. However, there are aspects on which their approaches meet. This is where the principles of A. L. or Accelerated Learning were born.

Combining different methodologies from different areas of

specialization would seem too complicated for an individual aiming to go for self-initiated accelerated learning. This is the reason why this book was conceptualized and put together. Every aspect of accelerated learning will be discussed in the simplest manner possible.

Techniques that are proven to boost memory, improve learning efficiency and effectiveness, condition the brain for learning, develop study habits, and improve overall academic performance are included in this book.

It is hoped that through the use of this e-book, grasping the principles, concepts, and techniques of accelerated learning will be easy for anybody to do.

Thanks again for purchasing this book, I hope you enjoy it!

Chapter 1: Fundamentals Of Accelerated Learning

Accelerated learning or A.L. is currently getting a lot of attention these days. This can be explained by the fact that from a collection of concepts and research-backed principles, a lot of impressive practical applications can be derived out of it. There are many pieces of scientific literature already written about this as of present time. While the explanation about AL may vary according to who is talking, it could be explained in just a simple line. Accelerated learning is the most cutting-edge collection of theories, applications, and strategies that is aimed at boosting the speed and quality of learning. Yes, AL principles are backed up with huge quantities of hard data that were derived from years of research. An individual with a capacity to learn at speeds above the standard figures will have a better shot at achieving career success. There are many organizations and entities in the education and business sectors that have benefited already from the results of accelerated learning programs.

There are education and learning laws and principles currently seen to work just fine for individuals. The thing that separates AL from the traditional methods of learning is that it harnesses the latent capacities of the human brain. Traditional methods leave a lot of room for wasted learning opportunities. AL effectively uses these rooms to maximize the rate of learning that an individual could achieve. The multiple intelligence utilization approach of AL means that the process will include use of physical activities, music, sound, tactile materials, and other related things. By optimizing the environment where a learner is in, more positive results can be achieved.

Based from accelerated learning principles, an optimal environment is one that is:

- **Rooted on positivity** – This is because a positive

atmosphere relaxes and stimulates the brain of a learner. An individual will learn best if he or she feels a sense of safety, wholeness, and freedom to enjoy in a specific area or setting.

- **Allows active involvement** – Knowledge is best gained when an individual has a participatory (active) role in a learning scenario. A spectator's (passive) role can reward an individual with knowledge but only to a very limited extent.

- **Gives way to cooperation between learners**: The cooperative learning strategy as used in the current curriculum of educational institutions ensure higher quality of concept and knowledge formation among individuals.

- **Options for learning are varied**: There are many learning styles among individuals. The learner should have the freedom to choose his means and ways to grasp knowledge and skills. Each option should match the learning style of an individual.

- **Offers application of learned knowledge and skills**: This is called learning in context of use. Opportunities that are used in real-life scenarios are remembered better and longer.

- **Results-driven and gives way to more challenges**: Learners are always made aware of their goal which motivates them to boost up their efforts. When an individual has clear goals set right from the start, clear methodologies can also be prepared and followed.

Those who are planning to make use of the accelerated learning system must stick to its seven guiding principles. These are as follows:

   Principle #1: Learning process should involve both mind

and body.

Principle #2: Learning is all about creation and not absorption.

Principle #3: Learning happens best when there is collaboration.

Principle #4: Learning is a multi-process system.

Principle #5: Learning works through the input-process-feedback cycle.

Principle#6: Learning is a direct result of positively reinforced emotion.

Principle#7: Learning results from the image processing power of the human brain.

If we will look at the bigger picture, accelerated learning is like standard learning shifted to a higher gear. There are unconventional practices that rooted out from the introduction of AL into the normal learning systems we are used to. Examples include the use of classical music in a classroom setting, meditation before reading through lessons, and the use of mnemonic memorization tools.

If you need to learn the methods of this learning system, you are reading the right book. The next chapter will discuss the first and most basic part of the AL system...the human memory. Read on and start your journey towards being an "accelerated learner"!

Thanks for Previewing My Exciting Book Entitled:

"Accelerated Learning: Best Accelerated Learning Tips To Improve Memory And Speed Reading, Enhance Intellect And Brain Power, And To Learn More Faster!"

To purchase this book, simply go to the Amazon Kindle store and simply search:

"ACCELERATED LEARNING"

Then just scroll down until you see my book. You will know it is mine because you will see my name "Mick McPherson" underneath the title.

Alternatively, you can visit my author page on Amazon to see this book and other work I have done. Thanks so much, and please don't forget your free bonuses

DON'T LEAVE YET! - CHECK OUT YOUR FREE BONUSES BELOW!

Free Bonus Offer: Get Free Access To The PotentialRise.com VIP Newsletter!

Once you enter your email address you will immediately get free access to this awesome newsletter!

But wait, right now if you join now for free you will also get free access to the "LIMITLESS ENERGY" free EBook!

To claim both your FREE VIP NEWSLETTER MEMBERSHIP and your FREE BONUS Ebook on LIMITLESS ENERGY!

Just Go To:

www.PotentialRise.com